On Death

An Essay

Caleb Gattegno

Educational Solutions Worldwide Inc.

First published in the United States of America in 1979. Reprinted in 1985. Reprinted in 2010.

Author: Caleb Gattegno

ISBN 978-0-87825-246-6

Educational Solutions Worldwide Inc.
2nd Floor 99 University Place, New York, N.Y. 10003-4555
www.EducationalSolutions.com

Table of Contents

Preface

The meaning of this essay can best be described by saying that it aims at making me understand my place in the universe better. In so doing, others perhaps will join me, retaining from their reading that indeed, for them too, that is the case.

I believe the treatment given here to the subject of death, although brief, is of the kind scientists are proud of. Unsentimental by design, it does not concern itself with the irrationality of death, nor with the fears its existence generates in so many. Instead, it uses the light of energy and its transactions, as known in the various realms of our universe, to come up with a suggestion that makes sense to me.

I must have been very close to finding that suggestion over the last forty years, but it never hit me forcibly, demanding serious consideration, until recently. Two years ago, in an incidental remark to someone, I heard myself formulate it. For months the words returned to me but I did not let them occupy their space in my consciousness. Other matters were keeping them at bay, at least during my waking hours. During my sleep it must have been different, for, one day, I found myself in possession of a full blown theory expounded for the first time in the pages that follow. The crystallization that ensued assured me that I had struck a rich seam and that I had solved, to my satisfaction, an epistemological problem I had had all my life. Indeed, is there any hope that we may ever know what death is? Since it is a problem of knowing, we need to find the epistemological devices that will lead us to coming closer to it. I think this paper has something to tell on that matter — something useful and perhaps significant. My own way of being convinced of this is to be found in the liberation my theory brought me, I was freed from having to carry the tension the problem had generated in me.

More than this, the quantum theory of this essay served me well in other fields and allowed me to round some corners. It also brought more light into matters I had known required it, although not knowing before where to find it. The fertility of this theory therefore, goes beyond the scope of the essay and may serve to recommend it to those investigators who, like me, prefer wide issues.

I would like to end with a few words of thanks to Charlotte Balfour for her work on my English, to David Wheeler for earlier stylistics remarks, to Yolanda Maranga, my secretary, for the care she took in typing the text for reproduction and to Clermonde Dominicé for readying the material for publication.

C. Gattegno
New York
November 1978

1 Introduction

I have lived through the deaths of many people; my parents, some of my brothers and sisters, some relatives, some friends, some neighbors, and many, many unknown people killed in a number of wars, accidents, and epidemics.

But I have not yet lived through my own death.

Whatever I end up saying in this essay On Death may perhaps turn out to be very far from the reality of death itself, which I cannot even be sure of knowing when I am dead.

Thousands of writings bear witness to what thousands of thoughtful people have found about death in the process of their experience as living people. Why then contribute more words and ideas to this field, closed as it is to our conscious self? For years I have hesitated to express myself on this matter, although knowing its significance in my present life. In it I have been privileged to dwell in many important challenges, rather than be totally absorbed, as so many must, in facing the needs of survival at every moment. Because I have had time to study myself in my concern with death I may have come across some light which my readers may find to their liking.

In my case two things are certain, it is not my purpose to alter the reality of death in order to allay some fears of mine, nor do I seek satisfaction from writing this essay in that people may find it interesting. I have lived consciously with the impact of death since September 1918 when my father suddenly died, and it took me many years to recover from that shock, the meanwhile registering the demise of other beloved ones.

I questioned myself with much passion about death and found little to console me or to enlighten me, only material to interest me and to warn me that, maybe, we are all in the same predicament: only able to speculate about it. In fact, only when I agreed to remain forever ignorant of it did I feel that I might get somewhere, while when deeply involved in it I only experienced the mystery of it and a helplessness before that immense, closed world.

People consulted me. When they were grieved and shocked, they wanted to make sense of what they had previously met only through projections and beliefs. They expected me to tell them something which would take care of their present inner state, not really to tell them where I was concerning the matter of death.

People who had heard me speak of "this life" and occasionally say something of "other lives" — which I (jokingly) spoke of as if they were known to me — would expect me to remove their doubts and justify their hopes of being once again with departed loved ones. Needless to say I was not of much help, simply because, like almost everybody else, I felt baffled by the "phenomenon of death" and grieved sometimes when those I knew died.

It became clear to me that I used the word death in a number of meanings and that I shifted from one to another, sometimes without even noticing it. I therefore made myself be watchful and keep all the meanings in their respective places, watching also how they affected one another. I studied my instruments of study so that I could assess, as truly as possible, whether I was making any progress in my grasp of the challenge.

I remember that for 39 years I had wanted to know precisely what sleep was and all the time its meaning escaped me — and all other students of it as well, I think. I did, after all that time, find a meaning for sleep which enabled me to say that I had answered my own question satisfactorily. Others agreed with me when they read my writings on it, or when, in seminars, I put to them the exercises which they needed to go through in order to know what I knew and to become students of sleep in their turn.

For 60 years at least I have been engaged in the study of death and have experienced all along that, like sleep, its real meaning kept escaping me. Since I had managed to give myself an entry into sleep — which produced the state accorded to scientists when they solve a riddle of the universe — I was free to move to some other challenge. I never considered death as prolonged sleep because this did not seem to help much in understanding it. Indeed, what finally helped me understand sleep was that I sleep so often and could conjecture a function for those hours in which my self gave itself the conditions for performing some functions which need that state and no other. In order to understand sleep it was necessary to not give to the waking state the exclusive significance I had at first given it. Also, since I had denied sleep a significance equal to that of the waking state, I could only progress if I integrated both into a new entity in which each had its own relative significance.

The convincing feature in my understanding of sleep came from that organic integration of both (sleep and the waking state) into a new wider entity which could become one or the other under certain circumstances and at the same time illumined both. Sleep needed the waking state to become itself, and vice versa. Consequently many old observations gained their status as truths, many new findings resulted from this integration which became for me the true frame of reference of human living and of life in general.

Today, I ask myself why I postponed looking at death in a similar manner for so many years (at least 10), since I myself would ask participants in my seminars on sleep: "Do you die when you fall asleep?" — linking two unknowns to extract the reality of one, that of sleep, while leaving death untouched.

Today, I can only say that I did not then pursue the connection between sleep and death and that I do not as yet know why.

Perhaps it was the difficulty of constructing a succession of lives as well knit together as the succession of day and night are when related to the two states of consciousness met when one is awake and when one is asleep.

Perhaps it was the immediate intuition that a single life could serve as a receptacle for the latter succession while nothing similar presented itself — to me or to anyone else — as the context for a succession of lives where the experiential character could be found as easily as it was in the challenge sleep-awakeness: to know the other when one knew the one.

Perhaps it was that I had disciplined myself to look for the instruments of study within the challenge itself and that death, as a challenge, escaped me. I could only reach it, as stated above, as an outsider, and for that situation I had only "an existence theorem" i.e. I could reach an understanding of the existence of the state of death in others. People would know how to tell that I was dead because of one or other of the criteria used today to deliver "a death certificate." But this did not necessarily mean that I would know that I was dead.

This is for me, today, the challenge of death.

It is impossible to say "I am dead" when one is dead because the I who would say it is only defined by "I am alive" or "I is alive and only alive." There is no I outside the circumstances which condition the awareness leading to its affirmation, and these in turn can only define life. This logical circle binds me within its limits, preventing me from breaking out of it. Perhaps we must drop wanting to know death by the processes that lead only to life.

Still, it is a living person who is preoccupied with death and aims at sorting things out in such a way as to know that what he (or she) is in contact with is truly death, the death which negates life, even if death is much more than that which we have found can be negated in our life.

Just as only in my waking state can I write this essay — on which I can work both in sleep and the waking state — I can accept that only in the state of being alive can I write about death. This capacity to consider death in life does not detract from the sui generis reality, of death. The dead do not write — except in some stories that living people tell. Therefore the dead do not write about death. The sleeper acts through his waking alter-ego to convey what cannot be conveyed in the first state, but can in the second. Perhaps the living can write about death as it is, provided it is acknowledged that the broader entity which integrates life and death represents both when manifesting itself in one.

This is part of the challenge of knowing death: that people expect the dead to do jobs that only the living can do. This expectation, being vain, increases the mystery of death; but the fact that the job cannot be done in death makes all statements made by the living subject to caution.

Still, I, alive, am writing for other living people about death, at the same time I wish death to sanction my message as true although expressed in terms that make sense only in life. This is another part of the challenge of knowing death.

In knowing life we come across a number of visions. Are they all equally useful or useless in assisting us in knowing death?

When we accept, for example, that “breath” inhabits us when we are alive, and say that it leaves us at death, we can only account for the onset of death and for lifeless corpses. This does not add anything to our understanding of life or of death.

The challenge of understanding is complicated further by the secret hope that if death were truly known to us we could perhaps escape it and live forever. Here I shall avoid this trap, and concern myself mainly with what will bring us nearer to grasping the fact that death and life are two aspects of our condition, should that be true at all. No effort will be made to salvage anything, to protect values held a priori or to engage in choosing between the various views held by authorities, from antiquity to today, or put forth in the various religions.

A few years ago in an initial plan for an essay on this subject, I allotted some time to looking into the various proposals on death found in the literatures of the most prominent cultures. This I shall not include here, as it seems today that a more concise form of writing is preferable and that an historical approach would dilute the study and add nothing to it, or very little. In fact, since the literature is available anyone interested can turn to it. Hence, without loss to my readers, I can restrict myself to what is my personal contribution. That, in my view is the only justification for writing this essay.

2 Individual Quanta of Energy

We have learned from physics that energy exists in various forms which can be transformed one into another. We have also been forced to involve energy - in "closed systems" - in two transactions that have been named the "conservation principle" and the "entropy principle." The first states that energy can only change form but cannot increase or decrease in quantity. This makes total energy a constant in a closed system. The second principle states that the quality of energy in a closed system tends spontaneously to change its form into that of heat, heat which takes a lower temperature all the time until it eventually reaches the zero absolute and remains forever in that state, unable to produce any further transactions.

Thus, in a closed system, a given quantity of energy is able to take any one of the various forms we know it under (electric, magnetic, mechanical, gravitational, chemical, radiation, heat). But, in assuming a new form, in every case it produces some heat, which spontaneously lowers its own temperature more and more until it can go no further — this state is labeled the zero absolute.

All our studies of physics have confirmed this fundamental vision of energy in a closed system.

When a system is <u>not</u> closed two things are possible. One, the total amount of energy of that system can be varied in plus or minus in transactions with another system whose energy affects that of the first. Two, when energy from a larger system is passed on to the one we are considering, the inevitability of its running down is inoperative and the system may end its transactions with more, and not less energy than when we started looking at it and either keep the temperature constant or even make it go up.

It is clear that we can consider wider and wider closed systems in which the two principles obtain. A system such as our <u>total universe</u> has been postulated as inevitably running down, and the "death" of the universe as equivalent to the automatic end of an entropy system which takes place through its ultimate inability to raise its own temperature above the absolute zero. In other words, an infinite amount of energy would be required to keep the system going, and the sum total of the energy in the total universe in all its forms is conceived of as finite.

Physicists have accepted without question that the magnitude of the closed system does not affect the way the two principles operate i.e. the conservation principle is to remain valid at all scales and the entropy principle as well. Within this frame of reference they have produced all the technology we find around us today, technology which includes both minute electronic transactions between atoms and vast nuclear explosions of almost unlimited extent.

The users of the energy systems surrounding us know that a battery is used to make computer chips function and that they must buy a new one after a while because they run down. They also know that they must plug in their shaver or toaster or refrigerator to get it to function for the purpose for which it was created.

The complexity of thinking required here is caused by our having to consider energy systems of various scales as having two possible states — isolated or connected — and these as functioning differently according to whether there is energy flowing into the system in both states, or only when connected.

In 1905 Einstein made physicists consider that matter was energy. This was a breakthrough in our thinking because matter and energy struck physicists' minds as well as their instruments in such different ways that they could not conceive of both as one. For Einstein and all physicists since, the principle of conservation of mass (postulated by Lavoisier around 1780) became a special case of the principle of conservation of energy (postulated by J. R. Mayer and by Joule around 1840). Because any mass (in grams) is quantitatively a certain amount of energy (in ergs) divided by the square of the speed of light (in CGS units), the only change available in the cosmic universe is from energy to matter and from matter to energy (in its form of gravitation and of radiation) in terms of $E=mc^2$. Heat is generated at the same time as matter becomes energy; energy in the form of photons and energy needed to propel these into space. The heat generated marks the presence of the down trend factor of the entropy principle.

As long as the physicists could see that the two principles were fulfilled, they could inject energy from one system into another and increase the variety of usages of it in our environment. For example a car appears to be almost entirely matter until it is started; it then shows movement of that matter because it has a complex engine (entirely matter) made to transform the chemical energy stored in the molecules of the fuel into mechanical energy; at the same time heat is dissipated into the car and the environment. The entropy principle expresses itself in that that heat is as useless in effecting motion of the car as it is inevitable in these transactions.

A digital mini computer uses very "small" amounts of energy to function but more than is "needed" for its functioning because of the inevitable loss in heat which accompanies the transaction from chemical to electrical energy in the chips and the wires. Smallness is experienced because of the scale of our human mechanical operations, e.g.: winding up a watch, taking food to our mouth, keeping our eyes open, getting up and walking etc. Even among the various activities which require energy, there are differences felt by our sensory systems that tell us what scale is to be mobilized, to open a jar for instance, or to affect our lips to utter a word. By becoming aware that all day we are an energy system, producing energy transactions which sometimes use energy already in the system and sometimes utilizes outside energy, we prepare ourselves to understand a number of complex daily involvements, and this may serve us in this paper on life and death.

I have expounded in other writings what we can do with such awarenesses and I shall limit myself here to what is indispensable to my present purpose.

Biologists have done a number of jobs that can serve us. They have been able to pinpoint numerous chemical reactions which take place in the cells of unicellular and multicellular organisms. They are adding every day to our understanding of what is happening at the local level of molecules occupying the space of a cell. They can, every day more accurately, estimate the amounts of energy needed for each chemical and chemico-physical transaction at the level of molecular biology. Already for a century and more they have been pinpointing — at the scale of our soma — what goes on in the biological functions of breathing, digesting, assimilating; distributing energy through the blood and lymph; controlling through the nervous system, moving our body or limbs etc. i.e. all the energy transactions that require our system to be linked to a larger one capable of supplying all the time, or from time to time, the amounts of energy needed to actualize the transactions and the functionings.

We now know a great deal in that field, and we may be closer to finding what that knowledge can do for us when we take energy as our starting point in looking at life and death.

Biologists describing the phenomena associated with conception tell us that from the outside they see an ovule being released by an ovary into a space apart of the female reproduction organs, to permit it to meet spermatozoids, if these are present and still capable of breaking through a molecular shield and so produce a fertilized egg.

This biologists can study. They can also tell us that for a number of hours the fertilized egg floats and moves towards the uterus to find a place to implant itself, while a process of subdivision of the initial cell takes place, producing a multicellular organism. Once implanted, that isolated energy system becomes attached to a larger energy system which for months will provide a supply of energy to assure the growth in utero of the embryo and the fetus. This also biologists can study and describe accurately.

For our purpose here, there are two moments of particular importance to be dwelled on more precisely.

One is the quality of the energy of the ovule and the spermatozoids which makes them capable respectively of being fertilized and of fertilizing. It has been established that only for a certain time can the two cells that are to meet produce the fertilized egg. This quality disappears thereafter and the ovule and spermatozoids then hold on chemical energy, which means that they are organic matter playing the same role as other organic matter in the female organism but not that of reproduction.

Another is the fact that for a while the fertilized egg is an isolated energy system (chemically speaking) and is already transforming its potential energy into that of the links between molecules which form the various cells in the zygote.

Hence, from the moment of fusion of the gametes and for some time thereafter, the biological energy of the system (accessible to biologists) is one that is distinct from that which can safely be termed purely physico-chemical — as it would be if the gametes failed to fuse — and it therefore belongs exclusively to the new organism.

It seems safe to assume that this distinctive quality of that energy is the element which, pertaining to that individual, enables it to survive till it procures for itself the energy it needs for growth.

By pointing at a quality of energy rather than at quantity we bring a new element into the picture whose significance and importance will only be known when the actual consequences are made explicit.

Besides an understanding of the actual transactions of chromosomes and genes between the two gametes which allows us to account for a lot of what goes on in the months of gestation after an egg has been fertilized, there is something in conception that allows us to make a new start and, while not touching what biologists will go on finding, allows us to account for what biologists have not yet attempted to find.

Evolution becomes a reality after we have conceived of it. It makes possible the linking of generations and can be extended back to the origins of the cosmos, to the creation of all atoms and all molecules and, after a jump, of life and its two main realms; the vegetable and the animal. The complex universe we are in and which scientists have managed to study in such detail is still more complex than we know how to convey yet, since man's evolution is intermingled with his view of the evolution of his universe. Every correct intuition transforms our vision of the world, and forces students of reality to alter their outlook.

An intuition of the moment of conception as being the descent of an energy — unique in some quality resulting from a property recognizable in the two gametes which have fused together — into the fertilized egg, while leaving all we already know to be true untouched changes our possibilities of understanding what has escaped us so far.

We are asking our readers 1) to conceive that there exists, besides its quantity, something we have called a quality of energy, which accompanies it and determines the time during which conception is possible, and 2) to conceive that it is this quality that will characterize the individual from then on. The ongoing achievements of evolution are available from then on to provide the individual with all he needs to reach the moment of birth and come into the world outside his mother. We want to concentrate on the moment of conception, and to keep in view the fact that the energies of the gametes possess a specific quality, needed to produce the inception of a new individual.

Not only do we see energies coming together at conception but also the generation of another energy which is quantitatively sufficient to direct all the processes that are available through evolution and through the energies brought in by the mother's blood to produce a unique human being. * Every human being is endowed with a unique quantum of energy at the inception of its life. Quanta of radiation, which have a quantity $h\upsilon$ of energy associated with them, have a quality which resides in the uniqueness of the integer υ characterizing a quality that man calls color.

The quantum, quality-quantity, being energy, can transact with all forms of energy and is not a metaphysical entity. It can discriminate between forms of energy and the qualities which make each item into: an atom, a molecule, a chemical reaction, a photon, a current of electrons, a chain reaction, a structure, a tissue, an organ, or a complex of any of these, and all the energy flows found in the soma at any stage of development and through all the phases of integration and subordination met in growth.

By allocating to each of us at conception a unique quantum of energy we separate the processes of heredity and nurture from the function of a self which is capable of riding these processes to make them produce what is needed to be in the world and to have a unique life through them.

---

* We leave to our readers the extension of these considerations to animals or even plants.

This quantum can at least account for variation.

We separate this quantum from all the other energies, but do not deny it the fact that it is energy.

By making it a quantum and above all a quality of some energy, we do not burden the newly formed egg with attributes that make it unwieldy and a priori mainly capable of making explicit what our imagination expects from "facts." What matters is that it exists, is unique and knows itself as energy and as such is capable of transacting with all the forms energy has in our world.

What we are drawing attention to is that by only calling on a personal quantum at conception we have given ourselves an instrument we did not have before, and it may prove to be a sufficiently powerful one to solve problems we could not have dreamed of tackling without it.

This quantum which is me at conception is the only item not having the form of objectified energy found in the many molecules of the ovum and the far fewer molecules contributed by the miniscule spermatozoid that reaches the nucleus in the ovum. During the floating hours of the fertilized egg, this quantum is independent and autonomous and directs the division of the cells and their arrangements using the energy available in the egg, asserting its total command of the subdivision being produced. From the available energies, the self (a new name for the quantum once it is at work) discriminates between those to which various functions will be given. In the restricted field of one and soon of a few cells, it will learn its job of director using every opportunity to make energy become matter, and that matter takes various forms, and all the processes work with the minimum of energy required for their functions. Since the egg is a complex of molecules already endowed with energy in the ovary, there is as much energy as the self needs to do its jobs, and it does not need to increase this amount. All it needs is know-how. It learns this in the few transactions it undertakes with the total energy available in the isolated system.

When the egg implants itself the supply of new energy is comparatively inexhaustible. The self then does not need to do more than direct and use that energy for the purpose of generating a living soma connected with the whole of evolution, for which the nine months in utero are "the time of gestation."

The quantum (we give ourselves or find ourselves having) at conception, being that minute quantity that accompanies the fusion of the gametes, is never experienced as energy distinct from what the self does in time over one life, whatever the length of the latter. To find it we need a process similar to the one we are using now, whereby it can become a separate entity for the purpose of study or in order to solve a problem like the one we have given ourselves in this essay.

To the self in one life we do not need to attribute more than a know-how to reach all the energies needed to actually produce the manifestations that form all the appearances of life. Our soma is constructed in utero using the energies carried by the mother's blood; once we are born the air and the food we ingest provide us with more. The self's functions are subtle ones, always acting on differential quantities, while processes established at certain times do jobs requiring larger quantities and specific ingredients. The quantum, which is sufficient to orchestrate, survey and monitor organizations properly endowed in time with latent energies, is not felt although other aspects of energy are. The psyche and affectivity, emotions and feelings, expenditures of energy in actions, added energies through perception, all can be called in to account for the details of a life and for the description of living in this one life.

When the self becomes aware of itself, it knows that indeed one quantum is sufficient to go from conception to the end of one's life. To live is to exchange time for experience. The self has given itself all the equipment it needs to achieve this in the various layers of one life, or in other words, in the temporal hierarchies. In these layers we find in each individual unique ways of performing all functions, and in the aggregate of all these performed functions we note similarities and common features and, from them, generate heredity and the permanent part of what we call evolution. Since we can more easily know the functions than become aware of our initial quantum, we have accumulated a great deal more evidence of the objectified world, of heredity and of society, than of the energy of the self and its access to the sources.

3 The Quantum Dispersal

There are trees that are as alive today as they have been for thousands of years. Among them there may once have been some that have since been struck by lightning, felled by people, or attacked by pests. They cannot be said to have died, although we use these words to express the different state in which we find them now.

Because the earth, as a stellar body, goes round the sun in what we call a year, or about 365 times the time it takes it to go round its own axis or complete its day, we measure life in that unit.

Our "lives," as also those of all phenomena on earth including geological, astronomical and biological ones, are expressed in years and multiples thereof. We say the earth was formed about $4\frac{1}{2}$ billion years ago. We say that our galaxy, and perhaps our cosmic universe, is 18 or so billion years old. At once we ask ourselves, "What was there before that?" or "Can we expect to have a future as long as our past?" Such questions are legitimate only because they come to us, not because they have any meaning or can be handled adequately.

Looking at myself having lived so many years, why is it that I cannot say that I will go on living for that long again? Is it because that would make me 134 and only very few people live that long, or simply because in our world we believe in statistics and the census tells us that the average human life expectation is, in most countries, not more than 80 years? Do I give myself a momentum at conception that takes so many years to disperse itself?

In any case we must know that the duration of our life is a function of many components and that death means as many things as we can find at the end of our life. Not all of these deaths are equally difficult to understand.

It is, for example, clear that since I cannot live without air, if I fall into the sea and drown my death is not mysterious at all. Why I fell and did not manage to swim to safety may be a mystery.

It is equally clear that if I am caught in a fire and start burning, my chemical composition explains why my soma is consumed in the flames. My death is understandable as the result of my being combustible.

Similarly if I fall into a pool of sulfuric, nitric or hydrochloric acid, I can be dissolved simply because I made myself out of molecules of the universe and these molecules are susceptible of forming compounds with those acids in a way that transforms me and makes the organization of my soma disappear. My death is understandable because I am molecular.

If I fall from a considerable height onto solid ground I can rarely stand the mechanical rupture that the kinetic energy of the fall causes in my bones, my joints and my muscles, producing conditions that do not permit essential functions to go on. My death is understandable because I am a body like all other bodies, breakable like them and not viable if the unity required for functioning no longer obtains.

If I am attacked and wounded in such a way that one of the many links needed for functioning is severed, my death will be understandable. In wars, weapons are used precisely for that end, and we can understand why people die in such circumstances.

Likewise in accidents of all kinds.

If my assailants are germs and I develop a disease, my death is still understandable, although not as easily as in the previous cases as I may be equipped to handle their multiplication, which is the cause of the disease. If I am immunized — for whatever reason — I may avoid death. My survival may then not be understood as easily as my death would have been.

If I receive a letter and in reading it got an emotional shock of a certain depth and magnitude, I may die on the spot and my death will not be understandable. Likewise if I pass away in my sleep. There are deaths like these, and <u>they</u> are the ones that strike us as generating the mystery of death.

In fact, still greater mysteries are why I get old just because the earth goes round, and how death relates to age. We all have the visceral feeling that the young should not die and the old should. Does it result from our seeing older people die rather than young ones? Or from knowing intimately, but not rationally, that death is "natural" after a certain age and "unnatural" before another certain age? Infant mortality has been with us for a long long time, but we consider it a social ill rather than an inevitable statistical fact, and we are moved to do something to reverse the trend. In some places this has been achieved, confirming that that death was not "natural," in spite of its frequency.

Lumping all deaths together has in part created the confusion in everybody's thinking. When it is clear that there is not enough replenishing energy to renew the one spent in keeping the system going we can see death as the expression of that imbalance as soon as it reaches a certain level. When such deaths become avoidable through better organization and distribution of food supplies, we lose sight of their mystery, since we can postpone their event.

When it is clear that our energy system only functions between rigid limits on its physical and chemical conditions, we see death as caused by any trespassing beyond these boundaries and the avoidance of death as keeping within these limits.

Health and disease occupy our minds when we think of death; we believe that the first keeps us away from it while the latter takes us to it. Nevertheless healthy people also die and we have to understand their deaths.

If we assume that, however healthy we may be, the rotation of the earth, by a mysterious process, takes its toll, and being old entails a drain on the energy accumulated from conception in our soma and our psyche, we can see "natural death" as the moment at which the initial quantum removes itself from its position of direction and lets the rest of the self's energy return to the cosmos by cosmic processes. (Among these we shall count cremation and the exposure of corpses to scavengers.)

In such a view the self's initial quantum in each of us is the energy needed to do two things: first, to dwell in the psychosomatic system at the place of command and trigger energies left behind from the process of growth in the form of locked up energy in its objectifications and in the form of residual energy in the psyche and the physiological functions — these two energies have been integrated in time in the process of transforming what the mother's blood in utero and the food and air ingested after birth have brought to the individual, so that their supply is theoretically inexhaustible — and second, to energize the encounters with what comes (generally unknown) by concentrating on a pinpointed task representing this unknown. The quantum energizes by mobilizing existing energy in the psychosomatic system, producing what may be called our affectivity.

The self, therefore, rather than being a source of energy, is that small amount or quantum that can use the amplifying mechanisms that the reserve energies and the locked up energy in the psychosomatic system represent, to achieve the purpose of any activity.

In the process of growth from conception, minute amounts of energy are dynamized by being maintained in the midst of larger amounts. The numerous automatisms formed over the years require very little energy to function smoothly and this by design and construction. The self therefore does not need much energy for itself, but does need the triggering amounts to set off other amounts which are appropriate in quantity and in form to cope with the challenges encountered.

We are surrounded by systems of this kind in our universe of experience. We know that pressing a button can make a huge elevator climb many floors, sometimes very quickly. Our personal expenditure of energy is minimal; that consumed by the elevator considerably larger. If the elevator were not connected to a source of energy which permitted it to counter gravity, inertia, and the difference in levels in its travel, there would certainly not be in the self enough energy to move the cabin.

The self's function is to dip into the store of energy and use it for its ends. For that function a small amount of energy seems sufficient. The more evolved the self the smaller the amount needed for the predilection functions to go on. So the initial quantum — residing in the egg and possibly of a magnitude just sufficient to operate the few subdivisions of the cell till it implants itself on the wall of the uterus of the mother — will not need to be larger, so long as the environment provides the energy supplies needed to perform all the processes that life requires. If these supplies fail, the needed energy will not be there, functions will be hampered, and the effect will be to produce either a stillbirth or a weakling. The stillborn child is a corpse, i.e. locked up energy only. The weakling is a self but has little energy in reserve to mobilize the locked up energy and to make it do what it would otherwise have done with more, so that it develops with social handicaps (noted by comparison with others). It is therefore in life and not by death that we recognize that the quantum may be unable to command the supply of energy to do what it does for most people. There have been weaklings who have lived a long time because the environment has catered to them and made the extension of functions possible through care. Crutches and wheelchairs, for example, diminish the need to mobilize parts of the self that are only able to respond to a limited extent to the existing will and the link between the self and its objectified system of muscles and bones.

To come closer to this functional link between the quantum and the rest of the energy in the psychosomatic system, we may use the following examples.

Forgetting. We all forget. So, we can all find opportunities of being face to face with a gap where what was once energized is not now recallable. On the one hand we learn that the self hooks up parts of itself that we know now was reachable at one time: a formerly accessible track of some past event or experience — having subtle presence as if requiring very little energy to be maintained — was linked to the self, also subtly but in a determined manner, which is now obliterated. On the other hand we sense the duality of the searching self and the thing remembered, a duality fused into a continuous and undistinguishable whole which suddenly breaks apart into two components: one, the self, having as its present function to look for an item which it knows belongs to it — at the virtual level prior to the awareness that it has forgotten it — and the other, the forgotten item, — part of the self's objectified world. These two sensations which accompany the shock and the awareness that one cannot recall what was once one's own, may be fleeting and not of much help for our present research if the link is re-established and the forgotten item comes back, allowing us to pursue the activity we were engaged in when we met the gap in the supply of items from our memory. But if the breach lasts and we may engage in the study of what has happened, we may find invaluable help for our present search.

Indeed, in forgetting we find clearly the two components: i) the self as a quantum impressing itself as no more than a subtle light scanning a part of the inner universe; ii) an item known to be in that part of the universe and at present unable to come to the surface to be integrated with the rest of the now interrupted flow of mental items involved. Except for a certain distinctive quality recognized as being subtle, both components are susceptible to being acknowledged as subtle energy even if not labeled as such. By reaching this awareness: that retained items are mobilized subtle energies connected through subtle links to other subtle energies, we have access to the kind of association the self gives itself with the rest of the objectified world held in our system. The link with the automatic functions can be postulated as being of the same kind but as passing through the integrated hierarchy which was energized as it was made, in order to work smoothly.

We put items to be recalled and the objectified automatic self in one category, because they are produced in the same memory and remain at the service of the self; they are triggered at almost no cost, and make use of the residual energy the self has left behind so as to keep only the function of triggering for itself.

Since we can forget, we can find that the link is energy that will sometimes not respond to a call of the self to produce recall. Sometimes the self can use its familiarity with its own functionings to reach other links and rescue the forgotten item or to leave understanding of why the forgetting took place to another occasion.

Since we can forget, we see the unity of life become a duality (or a trinity, or something else): on the one hand, we experience the quantum of the self and, on the other, the work of that quantum that until now has led to the production of the energies locked up and of those needed to lubricate and maintain these energies, by taking them from the energy in the environment.

<u>Dreaming.</u> In my study of sleep I could find little to help me in understanding sleep so long as I attempted to give my consciousness in the waking state a preponderant and a prominent place. This at once made me into an intellectualist who could neither think of nor devise experiments to study myself, but only others.

The breakthrough in this case came when I knew that I needed to let the sleeper in me do the studying. Among the results which I established for myself, the one that can help us most here, is the capacity of the self to dwell or not to dwell in some of its functionings.

In the same way as we handled forgetting, we can handle whole chunks of our other functionings. The self that withdraws from the sensory endings no longer mobilizes the energy needed to convey the impacts of the outside world to the organized sensory systems which are educated day after day in our early childhood to recognize, sift, retain, etc., the energy of the impacts. So to "fall asleep" is to switch the self over from maintaining in contact with the senses the integrated system it has energized to being in contact with the energy left in the system — the energy that works within it for a few hours, i.e. the hours of sleep.

There are therefore two universes to look into. One concerns the switching on and off by the self of the contacts that trigger different, larger energy systems which were produced out of the energy integrated from outside day by day. The other concerns the workings of the self when it is in one state and not in the other. Some of us know the waking state quite well. Very few of us entertain sleep, the other state.

For our study in this essay the second state seems more helpful. Withdrawing from our sense endings is a well practiced functioning, since we used it during the first days following birth when the self was becoming acquainted with the outer world as an energy system and was learning how to cope with it. We are all experts at this switching. We have lost contact with the outside world, we have severed ourselves from it to return to the awareness of the state of the self when it is in control of all it does all the time, an experience it possesses because it has been doing this all the time since conception. Sleep is the true realm of our self because our inner world is of our making and the outer world is not. That our inner world is affected to a certain degree by the energy in the cosmos and in society, we do not doubt, but we are far less affected by its impacts than by the balance of what we retain, night after night or sleep after sleep, from these impacts.

Dreams are one of the activities of the self in sleep.

Because from outside we can observe REM (Rapid Eye Movements) we can be sure that the self has access to the energy that activates the muscles of the eyeballs and we can use this fact (in the waking state) in reflecting on what happens in sleep: that the dreamer affects some muscles selectively in the state of sleep. But observation stops there, and the research on REM requires that we wake the dreamer up to enquire from him or her what the matter was. When the supremacy of the waking self is no longer entertained, REM is no more than another item to be considered.

In sleep the self is as much at the helm of what needs to be done as when it walks or talks in the other state. Perhaps more so for some of us: because we can use the entire storage of experience available in the system from conception and do in continuity what in the waking state takes long periods of our life. Since dreaming is the only activity of sleep we transfer (be it only in part) to the threshold of wakefulness, we only know dreams as part of our sleep and in our waking state identify sleep with dreaming. Thus, not only do we now know, when awake, what sleep is, but we also delude ourselves into thinking that dreaming is what we do when we sleep, and stop attempting to know what the real function of sleep is, or even of dreaming.

Keeping in mind first of all the two presences at the moment of switching off or on, we see that we take into sleep the impacts of the outer world on us, and as we exit from sleep at the other end, we find ourself made ready to meet another day. We can see too that immediately after switching off, the self asleep has the huge job of sorting out all the impacts that it has retained as energy from the outside and also the energy delegated to the psyche, and see that this sorting out is the main function of sleep for us humans, especially in our crowded urban environments. But in coming back to the waking state, switching on to the outer world, we bring a self that may have learned its lessons by the self doing what was needed. That self was there the day before and received the impacts it received. It has worked many things out — for some of us everything — and now has to tell itself that what cannot be done in sleep has to be done in the waking state.

Because we have also kept in mind that dreams are the only activity of sleep that can linger on into the other state of the self, we must give to dreams the function of connecting the work done in sleep with the work to be done once awake. Dreams are functional in that respect. The self in sleep works differently from the self awake because in sleep the self is not restricted by actuality and works on energy amounts that are very minute compared to those needed for most of the activities of the waking state. This difference in scale makes the self in sleep much more powerful than the self awake because in one state there are very few obstacles to what one can do with the content of the system while in the other the obstacles of the environment are such that one may not have the means to surmount them all. The dreamer awake knows that he is doomed, but the dreamer asleep may well provide the self awake with what is needed to engage in the solution of problems. Dreams are messages from the self at work in freedom and with access to all its virtual past, to the self awake who can engage in actions. For our purpose, therefore, dreams tell us that in our lives we never leave impacts as they are supposed to be, the way the environment intends them, to educate and prepare us. Instead we work on these impacts in the light of the continuity of life and come back with a proposal that wakes us up with the command to take such or such steps since only in the waking state can action on the environment take place.

Often a dream needs to be interpreted. The fact that the command is not clear tells that the sleeper is still trying some things out in terms only of the reality within. If the affective component of the dream lingers for some time, the language of the outer reality is used to account for the images still left in our consciousness, and organized in terms of the life of sleep. The self when awake knows that something needs to be done and persists in reaching a meaning compatible with action in the world. When this happens the self asleep has served the self awake. When it does not happen, another night of sleep (or perhaps a few) will be needed to transmute what the self sees in one state into terms valid for the other.

Dreams are bridges between the two forms the self has to take when in contact with very different energies in the environment of the outer and inner worlds.

If we cannot be aware of automatisms in the waking state, if we can only be in contact with a fraction of our objectified world when engaged in the polarizing activities of the waking state, we have not asked to know ourselves in everything. If we cannot be aware — in the state of being awake — of what goes on when we are asleep we have not asked what sleep is, although we peacefully go to sleep every night. Being asleep and being awake are both part of life, and our self can restore the unity and integrate both by giving to the state that can act, the job of acting, and to the state of sleep, the job of maintaining health (somatic and mental) by sorting out things in the narrow environment of our human relations.

***

Because we all dream and because we all forget, we have innumerable opportunities to study how these two forms of being — presented to us by the phenomena contemplated — make our reality monistic and pluralistic at the same time, without conflict except at the artificial logical level.

The quantum of energy we have is sufficient to keep both our inner and outer lives going. Kept going through the very elaborate hierarchies that we produce day after day, in sleep and wakefulness, in order to construct the unique being each of us is. The locked up energies in our soma, the residual energies in between, all are integrated and subordinated so as to be triggerable by minute amounts of energy that give the signal at the right moment so that the desired consequences take place.

The vision of a quantum at work all the time would be confirmed by any study we might make of human activities involving the self. There is no need for more than that initial quantum because we are in the cosmos and have so much energy available. Supplying the organized system produced from the initial egg with the needed energy is no problem since there is an endless supply in the cosmic environment. Our collective evolution has taken the turn of doing more and more with less and less. Today we can conceive of a self endowed with a quantum of energy doing all the jobs that present themselves in one life, from the making of the soma (in utero) to the writing of this book now, or to the removal of heavy furniture on another occasion. Today we can see that at the real helm of every single human life, there is a self that has learned to use a chain of command to minimize the energy involved in carrying out every one of the orders it gives and to keep for itself the functions of evolution while giving to specialized systems the various functions that produce what becomes what we know as the appearances in our environment.

***

Death is synonymous with switching off the quantum from the state of being linked with the hierarchies in their present state of work to being free to join the universe of energy, the "energy-individuals" which constitute our cosmos, just as conception is synonymous with switching on that same quantum within the energy made available by the two gametes that fuse to produce the viable egg that became me in this life.

For our purpose in this essay we have not so far concerned ourselves with more than the quantitative aspect of the quantum of energy. This does not mean that other aspects are not reachable and we shall consider some in the final sections of this essay.

What this section offers is a vision of life that can make the living understand death as a phenomenon.

By noticing that we do not need more than a certain quantum to start the process which continues from conception on, we have made the dispersal of this energy situated at the helm a unique event which in itself creates the state which the living see in a corpse: the locked up energy and the energy in the interstices which can now go back to the cosmos (in our case the earth) whence they came, keeping the principle of conservation valid. One quantum of energy is not sufficient per se to upset any physical instrument that has inertia. So there is no hope of physically capturing the quantum which makes us what we are at every moment of our life, one of these being the moment of our death. But it is possible to make its reality perceptible to other selves (because they too have their quanta) through the form one self has evolved to meet the challenge of itself and of death.

That which constitutes a corpse returns to the cosmos, because all is energy in various forms. The quantum that constitutes the self also remains — as energy — in the cosmos, though not necessarily in the same form as any other already existing quantum, mainly because the quantum that is me, now, has done something to itself through the life or lives it has produced and manifests itself therefore as an individual evolving being in a world in evolution.

Until we understand what happens to a self in evolution it is better not to try to decide where our quanta go to when we die, for any answer will be a shot in the dark, perhaps going nowhere towards meeting the challenge of understanding death and the after death.

From this side of death, i.e. in life, we can easily ascertain to what degree the "quantum theory" expounded in this essay is convincing. I have no doubt but that the facts of awareness I have collected in this life make it overwhelmingly convincing. Since I do not look at death as an event which saddens people, but as a phenomenon intimately related to life, I see it as one of the two limits defining the duration of a life. I look too at the other end and see two gametes merging, and the beginning of a new life that I have managed to see as a unit integrated with the continuum of all our lives. The slant in my thinking that takes account of energy, the connection with my knowledge that there is an indefinite supply of existing energy in the cosmos, has led me directly to the perception that if the egg can be moved by a minute amount of energy to gain access to the energy supply around it, that minute amount (or quantum of this life of mine) is what will be dispersed when the link with the rest of my energy system is severed.

It is easy to see that, conscious of the link between the quantum and the means of experiencing, someone can choose to commit suicide, by any of the ways that cut off the relation to the cosmos: asphyxia (by hanging, by breathing gas in an oven, by drowning, etc.); bleeding profusely (by cutting arteries, by harakiri, etc.) destroying a vital organ (the brain or heart), or by starvation, etc.

But it is also easy to see that a strong emotional shock from an unexpected source can energize a center in the brain for a short while by releasing at the level of that center more energy than the self has in readiness to cope with ordinary demands in that area, and that the consequent loss of contact between the self and its nervous hierarchy is equivalent to a severance at the level of the helm. The quantum, instead of releasing itself, is forcibly released and the soma remains alone. Death has occurred, witnessed by the living, maybe not foreseen by the one who has died.

In old age, when the process has begun of not cultivating the presence of the self in activities of the past that no longer attract one, the self can dwell in all that which moves it closer to its beginning. The soma reduces — in some cases to a size that characterizes infants — as if the quantum wanted to reverse the process and reach the state in which it was before this life, perhaps considered at that time as a useless experiment in terms of evolution. Death of old age can be included among the pictures being painted here at this stage of our study (by a twist which may only blur the issue and not give us much that is of value) by saying that becoming old means that the links between the quantum and the energies of the objectified self become weaker for want of maintenance and at one stage are so weak that they separate, leaving the soma where it is and the quantum free to pursue its next journey.

As to death at early ages, we can see, for example, that malnutrition may not supply the energy needed by one's growth. Some selves are unable to find in the quantum how to remedy the situation while others manage to procure the needed energy, since only a percentage of the starving die. The quantum itself does not contain the required energy, but the self, through its cleverness or adaptability, finds the means of getting what is needed. The deaths of the young tell us that the quantum is only a director of energy, not a supplier, although it can direct the existing energy towards finding what to do with oneself and the environment, to reach the energy needed for the growth of the objectified self. That the young can die, tells us also that the duration of a life in years is not the measure of the meaning of life for any one of us. The quantitative aspect of the self may account for the way we can outlast adverse conditions in our life, but only a qualitative approach makes possible an understanding of what we actually do with our days between the moment of conception and the moment of departure from our soma.

To this we shall reserve the next sections.

4 Life and Death Reunited

My purpose in this section is to put myself in a state of contemplation of life where death remains at the center of my awareness. In the previous sections I tried to reach death from the side of life and I believe it helped me in finding a way to say things that I was not able to say before. Perhaps to find also what may be significant for others as well.

***

I was not quite seven when my father died. He died suddenly one evening, soon after reaching home, holding his right hand against his chest in the region of the heart. When he entered the living room, we were playing on the carpet. He sat in his rocking chair and said to my mother: "Take the children out." We (I cannot at this moment recall how many of us were there) were told to go to the dining room and wait there. I remember that I was filled with anxiety at seeing him in a state heretofore unknown to me and doing what he never did; sending us out, instead of playing with us, which was his usual joyous expression of being surrounded by us. The evening had come and the stars were shining brightly, the street noises were very few or did not reach us through the open window in that room on the fourth floor. I went to the window, looked up at the sky where I had placed the Almighty and said: "God, save my father's life and I'll give you one thousand pounds!" I had no trouble promising what I did not have and what, in my environment, sounded like so much. My prayer was a bargain. I did not think that God might be above that sort of thing. I wanted to express my need for my father as being greater than any desired wealth conceived of in the terms in which I had heard people around me speak. It seemed that God was too busy to listen to me and soon afterwards we understood that my father had died. We were not allowed into the room where he was. Instead, we were dispatched to various relatives, one here, one there, to spare us the sight of the funeral rites since we were so young.

A friend of my father's was so grieved that he rushed up and down the staircase crying out things incomprehensible to me except for two or three words that I can still hear 60 years later or believe I caught to be: "He was snatched from among us," — as if he had been taken by enemies. No suggestion that he might have died naturally. That to die was part of life.

That friend's white hair, and the esteem in which he was held in our household, made a tremendous impression on me. My father's demise was not only an economic disaster, it was also a mystery in which I found a place for myself as an accomplice of those who had snatched him from us. Indeed, a week or so earlier we had as usual gone to the park, where my father took us regularly. Fifty yards or so before reaching the front door of the apartment building where we lived, I dashed home, raced upstairs and knocked at the door out of breath. My mother opened it and asked at once with some surprise in her voice: "Where is your father?" Instead of using ordinary words, such as: "Downstairs," or "Near the main gate," I said in my excitement at having left him behind, something which meant, for me: "Far behind." But the words that I uttered seemed awful to my superstitious mother who at once slapped me across the lips and said: "Never say that!"

My mother was never violent and her reaction affected me very deeply. I did not understand what had happened but I felt it was terrible. When my father died a few days later I thought I had sent him there, to that far away place where I had said he had been.

My life from then on was to become complicated to a point which it is difficult to describe. I can say that I "matured" overnight in the sense that I saw that I had to compensate for the absence of my father, of which I considered myself to be the cause to a certain extent. I was a child, the last but one of 9 children, the oldest being 23, but I saw myself as having some responsibility towards the well-being of all.

It is easy to imagine the contradictions in which a destitute child can put himself by taking on the status of a father, while not knowing what that is. Playing as a child yet thinking about matters on which I had no grasp. I became the errand boy, I kept my mother company when she worked, lending a hand whenever possible, consoling her when she was in pain and cursing myself when she sighed and cried that he had left her with all these frightful problems which she considered to be his. I too, cried and in secret begged him to call me to him. I did not want to live. I had no one to share my secret guilt with. My involvement in life was intense and erratic. I had horrible nightmares which frightened me a lot in which geometrical figures moved fast and got huge and complex, with no way for me to stop them doing what they wanted. I could neither tell what my nightmares were nor get any relief from anywhere.

I was clearly a neurotic child, full of anxiety and fears, alternately acceptable and impossible, creating lots of questions for those around me who were naturally primarily interested in themselves and unable to do much for me.

At school I slipped to the bottom of the class. I did not study and did not do my homework. Bad marks were not received gladly at home since all my brothers and sisters who went to that same school had done well most of the time. I was considered an all round failure whose future was very much in doubt.

I have studied guilt from within, and for many years. I have watched myself and everyone around. I spent time mainly daydreaming, involving myself in wishful thinking of the type fairy tales are made from. I wished so fervently to get that instant wealth which I could hand out to my immediate family to compensate for all they were missing due to their father's death. “Their father,” I used to say, rather than: “Our father,” for I was to pay for my sins and they should not.

When people around us died I was not very moved. My imagination occasionally took me into an area where their grief became as real as my mother's, but I exaggerated my own situation and reduced to mere statements what was outside it. Since I had known my father's death, any other death was far less significant. On the one occasion when I visited my father's grave with my mother, I was so oppressed that I almost fainted. The feeling of extreme irrepressible anxiety caught me unawares time and again over many years when in movies or stories a father or a young child died, telling me clearly that I had not yet resolved the old complex.

All through my life I have remained with the feelings caused by the trauma of that event of September 1918. For eight years they affected my everyday life, until my adolescence when I suddenly realized what I had done as a child and how I had mortgaged my life on the basis of a single event which I had not quite understood. I saw that everybody around me, except my mother, had completely shaken off the effects of one man's death and I started to examine how I could restore my mental health by coming out of the complexes I had created for myself. Even then my life was still in contact with death.

Through all those years of work on myself I did not do the kind of work I talk of in the previous sections of this essay. I remained connected to death via the feelings and emotions my father's death had generated in me and although I have lived through the deaths of other dear ones, I have never again known death through life in the way just described.

***

Helen, a friend of mine, had lost her beloved husband after fifteen years of marriage and when we came to know each other a little better she shared her pain with me. Life between them had been so sweet, so congenial, that when he died her logic could not enable her to make sense of the event. She confessed that in a way she had lived with the illusion that it would last forever. Death had parted them and now she wanted to examine with me how she could fathom what had happened to him.

There is nothing logical in life or death yet a logical mind may be prepared to believe premises which meet its prejudices and preconceptions and move deductively on from there. Helen, facing the death of her husband, was going on living her life in the same house where they had lived happily together. She knew that she found him present in so many places, evoking him again and again doing this or that, or saying this or that. For her he was still alive, though dead, and she knew only with part of herself that he was actually dead.

The questions she entertained were about their possible reencounter. Daughter of a strict Protestant clergyman, she had rebelled against what he believed in and had wanted her to believe. So she was not prepared to imagine her husband in that stereotyped after death Christian world where one day she would meet him again. She wanted him very much, but as they had been before, and not at the price of turning back to her father's views which she knew she had rejected for very good reasons. She was ready to investigate other conceptions of the after death.

I had told her that for 20 years before we met I had been considering reincarnation and she wanted to hear about it.

At first I presented it grossly as a departure of the soul from the body to a Bardo (a word borrowed from the Tibetan Book of the Dead). But soon I was forced to look for a way of being more specific about this transmigration of souls. Where could I go to find more, and how could I manage the rigor her logical mind required and my scientific training demanded?

Death was lost in all this and became a moment in the contemplation of eternal life. Most religions had their answers and we looked at each of them. In every case there was something that prevented us from becoming convinced. We were asked to take too much on faith. As we did not manage to sort things out and as life was proposing other problems to us that occupied us both separately and together, we only occasionally came back to the challenge of life after death.

***

In the spring of 1963, I found a new entry into reincarnation when a little girl then 21 months old, whom I shall call here Pat, forced me to put the question in a new form: "Is there evidence that someone in one life acts in ways which cannot possibly result from the learning that has taken place in that life alone?"

Here are some of the highlights of this experience.

Pat born in October '61, seemed to have brought with herself a great deal that delighted and amazed her parents. She learned to speak English in England by choosing to speak it as the announcers of the BBC did on the radio. At home she had two parents whose accents were foreign, neighbors who on one side were Irish, on the other Welsh, and across the road, Swedish. It seemed that she had chosen her kind of speech according to aesthetic rules given her by her musical self. That was delightful but not too surprising. At 17 months she had, besides a good use of Hindi (her mother's tongue), several hundred words of English at her disposal which she reeled off in "perfect" British English.

She had given herself to language before attempting to get up and walk. The latter she attempted only at 14 months. So she used to sit a lot and to act as a sitting person. When her toys rolled out of reach, she would show initiatives compatible with her choice of mobility, often very clever ones. That was accounted for by granting her a great deal of intelligence.

One day at 20 months she surprised everyone by showing that reading English had made sense to her and that she had taught herself to read on her own simply by being present in the living room when her mother taught neighbors, five-and four-year-olds, using the materials and techniques of Words in Color. Once, one of the boys being taught was having difficulty reading a sentence. Pat addressed him: "Colin! have you lost it again?" and came to the wall and showed him the sentence made of words on the first two charts. Of course, she knew more than those words. On testing her it was found that she had assimilated the vocabulary on the first twelve charts and could do complicated sentences when words picked out from over the whole extent were pointed at.

Everyone was thrilled and she enjoyed the excitement.

One day soon after that, a guest came to that room. He asked about the materials hanging on the wall. It happened that to make him see what they were capable of eliciting from learners he could be shown what a child, not yet two, could produce in English out of a restricted number of words, Pat was fetched by her father. She was still small enough to be held in one arm, with the pointer in one hand and her on the other. Pointing at a word that Pat knew and had read earlier, on its own as well as involved in sentences she was invited to say it. She looked at the word, looked at the guest, looked at the person pointing and, simply and firmly said: "I don't know." She was shown other words and each time she repeated "I don't know." Bargaining with her she was told that one knew that she knew each of them and that she was not being cooperative. But she did not budge. She only said: "I don't know." After a while she was let go. The guest could have known nothing of what was going on in and among the people present, who resorted to explanations instead of the spectacular demonstration that had been foreseen.

For days I meditated on that event. I discussed it with Pat's mother who was very close to her and the obvious conclusion was that Pat had done everything deliberately. She had chosen to say: "I don't know," rather than saying anything at all for each of the words pointed at, as many students do in circumstances where they cannot read. She knew that if she stuck to: "I don't know" no one had a way of getting her to say the word and would have to leave her alone. Saying the word on her behalf would only have proved that one knew how to read it and, had she repeated it, that she could repeat words and not that she could let words tell her what to say, which was the purpose of the demonstration. By saying: "I don't know" she had the perfect weapon to make one abandon one's attempt.

What remained with me was that Pat had been brought in for a purpose, that she had seen a guest, that she had looked at the word, the guest and the person holding her, in that order and had refused to do what she had done several times before, though knowing one knew she could read what was pointed at. How a 21 month old child could assess a social situation of that complexity and select from among crying, talking nonsense or taking the pointer from one's hand and banging it on the objects around her, climbing down and running out, or anything else one can imagine, and instead say the irrevocable: "I don't know," remains a burning question. I found peace only when I had accepted that she was wiser than her father and loved him so much that she chose to enlighten him on the foolishness of that action and the damaging effect adults can have on children by wanting to exploit their gifts for other ends than their human growth.

I had for a long time thought that we reincarnate but I held that view as one holds a theoretical posture. Here I had tangible proof that the wisdom shown by Pat could not have been learned in those first few months of her present life and was what she must have brought with her. She could not have learned it in those 21 months because her present life was demanding a lot from every moment of each hour, and I had evidence of all that she had learned intensely and to the point of mastery.

I thought back to her choice of whom she would use as a guide for her English and marveled at her correct selection of the BBC rather than the more visible and steady environment represented by her parents and friends in the neighborhood. I worked on many of her learnings and found her a very swift learner using all her gifts to achieve her ends quickly and securely. I was satisfied that I had the proper instrument for my study of her, and particularly that my question: "What can a child learn by himself?" would yield all that babies and young children learn by themselves in this life. I made room for gifts, for nature and nurture, and they all produced satisfactory yields in my study of how skills are acquired and what babies do with their time at the beginning of life when left to themselves or when they relate to items of the environment or to the people in it.

But it never occurred to me that I could find an entry to further understanding of the meaning of what we bring from one life into another.

When wisdom and not skill is the subject of research we are helped in releasing ourselves from involvement in one viewpoint and in making room for another slant in our searching mind. That is what happened to me.

***

In the last fifteen years, and in some cases for even longer, I have allowed myself to gather whatever evidence I could encounter to work on the challenges of life after death and on that of the continuum of experience from one life to another. What I found to be valid may not seem much to my readers. For me it is a lot which would take a lot of writing to expound. Here I shall only discuss one point: "What is it that goes from one life to another?"

We all believe, naively, that what we retain in our memory is what we have learned. Thus people have entertained as proof of reincarnation recall in this life of events from previous lives.

I abandoned this view a long time ago. But I did not know what to substitute for it. My studies of the brain and of the relationships between body and mind had led me to place man's evolution in the mind and not in the brain. Man came into being on earth — that is my contention — when he became aware that he had awareness. The evolution of mankind is the story of that awareness of awareness. Although man is of the four realms and belongs to the atomic and molecular realms (1) as much as to the cellular (2) and the behavioral realms (3) he is essentially man because he is of the realm of awareness (4). From the first three realms he keeps those evolutions which extend over the billions of years that it has been calculated it took our galaxy to produce our present habitat on earth. So I see each of us as getting the benefits of those billions of years through the actual processes of transmission of structure, of energy. I also see each of us as an individual who, with the awareness he can use, gives himself a life on earth that permeates all that which is obtained from the other three realms and makes it unique, personal. As we saw in the previous section it is the quantum of human energy that directs its use of all that is in the environment and leaves the body behind as a witness to one of its works (development in utero first and in further physical growth after birth). Some of us leave contributions in other realms, such as our works of art, our tools, our books, our organizations, etc.

During this life I have watched my evolution and I can squarely say that what I have done for myself is to educate my awareness — in fact the only thing educable in me.

My self (and its quantum of energy which is its ultimate reality, making me part of the universe) has developed certain attributes. We manifest the attributes of the self in this life. One of them is the will, another is awareness. Hence, if we begin a study of the attributes of the self and find them co-existent with the self rather than manifested through its works, its objectivations, we can conclude: 1) that this is what our evolution in one life is, 2) that this is what we take away when we die, 3) that this is what we come back with when we start again almost from scratch, giving our self a form to express itself in among humans.

Since we are prepared to say that the forms of energy detected in our physical universe are one because they are all energy, and many because of some attributes owned by some forms and not by others, we may be prepared to give our quanta attributes which will make our individual human energy unique in some respects and universal in others.

The quantum that is the self can descend into one egg and do all the jobs imprinted in that speck of matter, summarizing billions of years of cosmic and earthian evolution. With these jobs which affirm our individual character because we do them from scratch (or almost) we give ourselves a form, a unique form, even if it "resembles" that of our parents and siblings. How we dwell in the form and what we do in utero with our mother's blood is more the outcome of the previous life (or lives, if we posit a chain of lives) and characterizes the newly born baby. What we do with the forces in the environment takes its character from our previous lives as well as from our present awareness of our experiences.

From our past lives we bring the state of the set of attributes of the quantum which allows us to enter our present individual life in a unique manner. Since lives are akin, we come into this life prepared by what we did in our previous lives to do everything which can be accounted for by biological and social heredity. It does not take much to be integrated into the group we are born into. We at once take advantage of all that is offered us. We immediately know what to do and reserve our unique features to give ourselves our unique life. Hence all lives look alike only if we concentrate on the attributes of the self which connect it to those forms of energy which are transmissible. For this we need no awareness of our quantum, the descriptions preferred by scientists suffice. Their theories too.

But when we allow ourselves to enter the actual individual manifestations which are unique to each of us we do not get much from this very general outlook. To get more we need an awareness of the state of the attributes of the quantum at conception. We need to inquire how we entered the egg, why we chose our parents, and what we did with our hereditary processes thereafter.

Before it was known that 400,000 spermatozoids were needed for one of them to fertilize one ovule, it was thought that mating took place for its own reasons and that sometimes, soon thereafter, the woman would be pregnant. Now that we have studied the phenomenon of fertilization of the egg, we are left with the question of: "Why one ovule and so many spermatozoids?" To gain some peace, we look for the attributes of an individual spermatozoid, and ask which of these attributes needs to be multiplied to permit one germ to implant itself in the ovule and fertilize it. We have made something visible in the phenomenon of fertilization in finding this large number of individual spermatozoids, yet finding that, generally, only one reaches the surface of the ovule. There is no visible reason why so many are needed but since the fact is there we must look for a justification for their number in terms of our comprehension of biological phenomena. For a while we can live with the fact, and with all the unconvincing theories about it. Until the proper attribute is suggested and found to exist, we live with whatever we can understand. Today we do not know how one quantum of human energy can integrate all the energies of the (first) three realms present in an egg to start the human deployment of the soma and psyche in utero. But we have a specific problem to work on in the way we feel we must to account for that large number of spermatozoids. Whether we invoke the existence of a quantum from outside the egg or not, we have the challenge of finding how the universal process of fusion of DNA from ovule and spermatozoid produces a human being. In my suggestion it seems that we take fewer assumptions to meet this challenge than biologists do.

Proposing that a quantum of energy descends into the egg when it is formed is equivalent to saying that each self selects its parents for the purpose of giving itself a form and an environment. During the growth in utero for which one has mainly selected one's mother, it is her blood that allows the soma to be made. The father's role is reduced to fertilization. But for the self ex-utero, the father again becomes important, sometimes, and in some societies, more so than the mother, after a certain age.

In a synthetic view of the whole of one life there may be some advantage in considering that each of us is responsible for what one does for oneself from one's beginning to one's end — when one's death is not due to an accident. That is why I take it upon myself that I have made my soma, I have chosen my mother and I have let the environment do so much with and to me. I shall be responsible for my death as much as I am responsible for my health and my diseases. My self gave itself the means to be on top of things in a number of areas, the beginning of my life proves this. The attributes of the self cultivated in one life permit, in the following life, the making of selections which may give it the environment in which it can dedicate itself to the pursuit of what these attributes make possible. Thus, one selects one's parents so as to give oneself the environment which will contribute to one's continuing evolution in the human universe which has been created collectively in a world of individuals. From my mother's humors I extracted a great deal that I have incorporated into my substance. All that which in her blood could be affected by those attributes of her self which were ones that I had valued in my previous life, I put into my own flesh in making myself within her. This made me better able to pursue my evolution, particularly since the environment in which I was to be born was in part affected by those same virtues.

Ex-utero I have to accept — because it is a fact of life — that I gave myself a set of conditions that challenge "me," i.e. my self and its attributes at this stage of my evolution, to force me to become aware of how to continue my evolution. My mother too had evolved in that environment (as most do except in a very mobile society needed to be considered separately) and her state at the time of my conception — which affected her humors, hence my environment in utero — affected me too and prepared me for meeting challenges in the world ex-utero. By choosing my mother I gave myself further chances to entertain what I had done to myself in my previous life. I gave myself the conditions for pursuit of my evolution.

In the complex environment into which I was born as an individual, I did what is compatible with individuality: I selected how events would affect me and which events I would let affect me. This choice is what certifies that I am in this life to do something connected with my previous life and that it is the attributes of my self developed in that previous life that I bring with me into this life, and not mere memories of events.

The fact that life in the fourth realm is human means precisely that the evolution of humans takes place at the level of producing the new and not in perpetuating the past, as in the non-human. Individual consciousness, constant selection of what is to be ignored and what is to be stressed, give to each of us the responsibility for our evolution by giving us an environment which challenges our consciousness and lets us choose to live this life in circumstances and in a manner which force an awareness of what is to be valued. The fourth realm is being created, generated, by the humans who accept not to do in their present life only that which takes away the potential of evolution in the individual. These humans show that what is taken from one life to the next is creativity as an attribute of the self, giving each of us the means (personal and environmental) to take steps in his evolution that will in turn allow other selves to come in with more chances to evolve available to them than could have existed before. The fourth realm makes collective evolution possible through individual evolution, and individual evolution easier because of collective evolution.

What we pass on from one generation of humans to another is not that which perpetuates the species (this belongs to the two realms of the vegetable and the animal), but that which breaks through more of the forms which hold us back in our evolution. That is why the true inheritance among humans is neither property, nor rights, nor institutions, but a greater chance of being more oneself.

The old man that I am is aware of the thousands of lives that have been needed to bring me to the threshold of what I am seeing and writing about in this essay. From one to the other I did not need to take care of what could be done easily by the working of cosmic, vital and behavioral forces, all of which has been well documented by chemists, biologists and other scientists through molecules, DNA, the family, religion and other institutions. But I needed to take care of what would make me benefit from the experiences in one life, and affect my quantum in such a way that potentially, in the following life, I would not need to lose time by not recognizing what was there that I could ignore from the start and what needed to be stressed, i.e. what I could best give myself to.

I can say at this juncture that I <u>know</u> that <u>I</u> have had many lives, that from them I have mainly learned to take care of my own evolution and that from this life I'll take away a more powerful quantum endowed with attributes acquired in this life, my previous lives having made that acquisition possible.

My biography, if restricted to telling what I did and when, will only be concerned with the cellulose of the film of my life. The substance of my life is that I have found it possible to reach new peaks because I have done something to myself at the level of awareness that is akin to what the quantum does to itself from life to life. At this juncture, if the quantum were to leave behind all the objectivations that can be energized at this moment by its workings, i.e. my soma, my achievements, my various manifestations, it would take with itself the real human gains of this life represented by the attributes which on my next return will make me notice more sharply some of the things I failed to notice this time and at earlier times.

I <u>know</u> that I had needed many lives to achieve the state of my quantum as it was when I entered this life, and that one unending life could not have achieved this, precisely because I am aware both of what I had done and of what I had not done up until then. Since in this life too I am aware of what I have done — and more at this moment of what I could not do — I have need of more lives to chisel my self, my quantum, further and make me more myself by making me more human.

***

I have now reached the point where I perceive life and death at the same time, as lives following each other, with death the aspect of unhooking oneself from the forms one has given oneself because these forms are not quite adequate for what one came to do this time. Unhooking in order to hook oneself on again in a more evolved human — one's mother — and in an environment whose attributes will permit the next stages of one's evolution.

In this life I have let so many coins run away from me which I could have held onto if I had sensed deep down that they were necessary to my evolution. In this life I have prepared for my next life and I know that my death has no other meaning than that of giving me the opportunity to attempt, in a new incarnation, to take on those undone jobs necessary to my human evolution towards a more human life whose meaning will become explicit by my living it.

5 Since Death Shall Come

Since it came to me that I need a succession of lives to evolve into a human being, and after that to make my humanity more explicit life after life, I recognize death as the necessary hiatus between lives and not as the final end leading to an unknown ever after.

Being earthian my evolution is known to be earthian and, earthian evolution, as I know it, requires a fresh beginning to allow the use of the self as we have seen it can be used in a human life and, in order to facilitate this, the capacity to create the corresponding new forms. It is necessary to end one life in order to start another one.

This is not a trivial or obvious statement.

In fact, when we do not have the vision of life and death given above and we are only aware of some aspects of this life — death's function is seen as being that of curtailing this life and death is hated by some therefore, and welcomed by others.

Moreover, if death is seen as the end we approach from this side, it is totally unknown and we fancy it as fearful or invent an after death which soothes us.

No after death offered, besides a reincarnation to go on with one's evolution, could really invite us to leave life freely, joyfully. When looking at this life we can merely feel either pleased to get rid of its pressures or sorry to leave its pleasures and comforts.

At some moment of wisdom we see that since death shall come we should prepare for it. In some cultures this means making a will, taking out a "life" insurance, designating one's substitutes if one has a position of responsibility (king, chief, head of institutions, etc.), or making arrangements concerning some other aspects of what goes on in this life so that it can go on without us.

But all this does not touch the fact that we die, nor tell us why. The living may be thankful for what someone did before dying, but that someone may have done nothing for himself or towards reaching the meaning of his death in his evolution. In the same way as with the continual alternation of night and day, sleep and wakefulness, we may be so fully absorbed by the one (usually the state of wakefulness during the day) that we miss knowing the other.

Man so far has developed a technology which makes living by night as easy as by day, and has found that as man he can eliminate the distinction either by learning to be equally active in a cave or mine (now lit) as in the open fields by day, or by organizing his life in shifts and by rotating those shifts. In his evolution he has come out of the rhythm of the presence and absence of sunlight on earth and found himself capable of having a meaningful life outside it.

In his evolution man has educated himself to find the true meaning of sleep in his total daily life and has restored to it the functions of which he could not be aware when only concentrating upon the waking state as he did for millennia: a vestige of his previous states in the remote past, when the various instincts forced him as animal to adapt to natural conditions. In his condition of being man — that is of having awareness — he could penetrate all his behaviors and either understand them and continue them (as for example when he provided himself with oxygen or a certain environmental pressure, when climbing to high altitudes) or experiment with doing without what seems necessary in the animal state (as when fasting or abstaining from mating etc.). Man, knowing himself as free of the tyranny of instincts, can extend his examination of what is compatible with this freedom and see his "nature" as needing to be looked into. He can give himself modes of living which replace his bents, tendencies, inclinations one by one, to prove to himself that his "nature" can be reduced in this or that. So much of what goes on in the world under our eyes is proof of this.

Aware of evolution, his evolution above all, man has given himself the freedom to intervene in and on anything he can become aware of. This is translated into the numerous civilizations and cultures he has produced on earth. Each one giving his lifetime to it, spans of time equal to generations, have been given to enquiring into and affecting some individual or collective behaviors one after another. These go to make the biographies of some men and the histories of some groups and are selected for what they have been able to uncover of man and of the potentials of awareness.

Wherever it has seemed urgent for the energies of a people to be directed and concentrated on some specific challenge, it has also seemed right to ignore some matters and stress others. Then, that people's time was spent to exchange it for such specific experiences as would focus collective attention on the requirements associated with individual challenges.

Individual evolution is therefore deeply affected by collective concerns made plain within the culture.

Any time leftover in some individual life because it could be spared by the collectivity, could be devoted to something else.

This dynamic makes us understand both the dominance of collective traits in groups and the role of individual deviance in presenting others with springboards for collective evolution. The individual who acts within the degrees of freedom compatible with collective restraints and constraints, but as an individual, is the spearhead of evolution for that group, producing variation on top of conformity to heredity.

So long as not a single individual comes up with any variation, heredity occupies the whole of the horizon and evolution comes to a standstill. Life goes on in conformity and maybe to the full contentment of those who adopt the patterns of living transmitted hereditarily.

But as soon as a variation is allowed to exist and later on to be expounded, a jump can be taken and evolution reset in motion within that group, or in a dissident group formed to move out of the area, thus consolidating the group's consciousness and producing a new culture. Buddhism and Christianity are examples of variations becoming civilizations; Zen and Mormonism their offshoots, separating themselves off to produce variations that have led to cultures.

An awareness is required to move one man to gain a new outlook on the condition of man. Awareness of a succession of lives as being similar to the succession of day and night has been part of Hinduism for millennia, and individuals and collectivities have adopted the outlook. Within this perspective, man's view of himself has meant that what happens to oneself is looked upon very differently in India than in lands where reincarnation is either given another definition (as among the Bantu) or is not considered at all (as in Christianity and western civilization).

Still, because “familiarity breeds contempt,” only those who challenge the meaning of what is current around oneself can revive awareness of why some things are supposed to be as people say they are. It is easy to take things for granted and remain unconcerned with what may have a much deeper meaning when one considers it carefully.

If a collectivity holds a view of an after death, which is believed in, any alternative view of death will find this an obstruction. Reincarnation seems to clash with the western view of after death, although in fact the two are such that they could be contrasted. Instead, reincarnation is looked upon as denying an after death.

What is said to happen after death is supposed to influence deeply what one does in life. This indirect effect is reached through the mind which holds explicitly that view in order to decide whether to act in this way or that. If we forget that we have been told that, we might end eternally in hell, we may act very differently than when we remember it. In some civilizations it is assumed that, somehow, people will not forget.

By contrast, an awareness of how one feels about one's thoughts and actions, of how one comes on one's own to consider what one has done or is doing, joins with the awareness of oneself as the doer, motivated from within and in direct contact with the power of modifying one's behavior. Looking at the life of one self as the testing ground in which to prepare oneself to bring oneself — through experiences and conscious experiencing — to a knowledge of the meaning of that life, restores to oneself the individual responsibility for one's action and thoughts. Reincarnation squarely sets on oneself the responsibility for one's actions, not to be judged by someone else who rewards and punishes. Reincarnation demands a higher ethical responsibility than the threat of eternal bliss or torture.

Moreover, what is lived concretely feeds back information about oneself that can at once be interpreted in one's awareness in order to know whether it is in harmony with oneself or clashes with what one knows to be one's best interest. Everybody knows directly, from very early childhood on and without the help of anybody or of any system of outside values, that one's actions have consequences. Due to this directness of experiencing, each of us has established safeguards which feed back to us the manner in which we should steer the course of our actions, related immediately to this life. From standing and walking as babies and accepting to fall in the process, we learn that our actions have consequences that may affect our future, a future which somehow resembles our present and past. But to aim at an after death unrelated to this life or exalting the pleasant sides of this life, is to detract from the importance of one's actions and from one's responsibility here and now, to adhere to a preconception which does not force itself on us in the way facts do.

We find so difficult to understand many of our actions and have had to produce so many theories to convince ourselves that, perhaps, we might look at reincarnation as another possible theory merely for the help this could give us in our effort to understand ourselves.

It is a theory which at the same time links life to death and birth. It calls attention to what we are doing with ourselves both to fulfill our outlook on life and to sort things out as they come our way so that we learn to live in greater conformity with the demands of life itself. Our personal outlook on life becomes meaningful, since the impacts of our environment would rather enforce uniformity than diversify. Whether this personal outlook is compatible with other people's outlooks or clashes with them, it comes with us and guides our choice of actions as a clearly individual gift. It is characteristic of who we are much more than our environmental or hereditary conditions are.

Aiming at fulfilling ourselves in life, we involve ourselves in thought and action, and that is what becomes our true biography. We determine our future in so far as we make choices compatible with what we brought with ourselves. We make it agree with the outlook we hold and only in part let it be a function of other impacts, such as environmental and cultural conditions.

The dynamics of actual living are not satisfied by looking simply at the model of reincarnation as the most adequate one available today. We all refer to temperament in order to understand ourselves and others, thus making an assumption similar to the one that we bring something with ourselves from before this life. Likewise, when we see our actions as having consequences beyond death. Only if we leave life and death separate can we be led to the belief that the reincarnation theory is nonsense. Any integration of death into life, bringing an inescapable end to it, will pose a challenge that reincarnation will meet better than can any after death theory extant today.

Particularly, a theory of reincarnation like the one put forward in this essay. A quantum allocated to each one of us, a minute amount of energy placed at the helm of the processes of life to direct them, using in an integrated way the additional energies extracted by it from the immense reserves of the environment and, at the same time, from the energy objectified by some of these processes.

Observing the dying has taught mankind everywhere that on the whole only an invisible "thing" will be missing when we do declare them dead. So, in so many places we evoke a breath, a soul, a spirit, as being the main difference between the living body and a corpse. That invisible thing has escaped all capture by gross means, the only ones available in all societies. A theory is the only way of objectifying a similar "thing" with its fingers or with a more subtle substitute therefore, like a photographic plate. A consistent theory is good — one that also identifies the "thing" at conception and follows it till death, better still. The quantum theory we propose here integrates evolution in one life and on the cosmic duration. It makes sense of death as one of "nature's" ways of working which can be turned to use for our benefit as were all those others we discovered in our local and universal habitat.

Once death is integrated into evolution it gains a new meaning, it poses other problems and challenges than when it was left separate from life and considered a disaster in some cases and a blessing in others.

For the individual who considers his own death, it becomes no longer the end, but only a necessary transition permitting a "new" start, a radically new start requiring another dwelling place and another set of instruments for expression and realization.

Let death come, not as a liberation from the pressures of this life on earth but as the liberation of what is "the essential one" so that it may come back with the means to start afresh so as to realize itself more adequately than it did the time before and, in meeting the unknown find the meaning of a complex life involved in complex and unforeseeable events. The meaning of living thus becomes: meeting what comes.

Being of the fourth realm means, by definition, integrating and subordinating what evolution has successively selected, of what has been tested, to be passed on in the other three realms — and tested for a proper way to use less and less energy for greater and greater ends. In such evolution what has passed on from one generation to another is: form, for plants; instinct, for animals; and for man, awareness. Form, instinct and awareness have always been considered to be qualities, attributes of energy and not energy itself. In our quantum theory it is suggested that the quantum be seen as the carrier of the qualities developed in one life and brought into a subsequent life to utilize everything that other energies have brought into the seeds or eggs, from the other realms. Evolution is seen as working on form, on instinct, on awareness and this alone is characteristic of what we are to look at anew. Rather than stressing similarities we stress differences and rather than finding the preservation of the species, and heredity, we find variation, the different, the new and by stressing it add to our insight into what we are: in detail, in any one life, and globally, over many lives.

Doing this has made sense of many things which look very mysterious otherwise.

In the same way as we pass from a night's sleep to the waking state — having resolved energy knots, excesses and distortions to prepare ourselves better for the following day — and from a day's activities to sleep — having received impacts of energy which leave traces of wear and tear on us showing our inability to cope with so much being poured on us by people and events — we take from one life to another the experience which our vigilance (or, otherwise, awareness) has enabled us to acquire in this life, so that the next time we do not pay so much heed to this or that as we did the time before or, conversely, are much more mindful of certain things than we were previously.

In an isolated system energy runs down; in a related system it can increase. What is increased or diminished is the potential of the quantum — a thing of the mind — not the bulk of the locked up or residual energy on which we draw for our activities, using our soma or our mind. That alteration in potential makes all the difference since we come back in a form already endowed, by millions of years of evolution, with the means to exist and to permit functions. That new potential results in a variety of awarenesses which can spontaneously take form because of this hereditary endowment. Thus it expresses itself in a total life rather than in a single feature which is easy to notice and classify. The objectified quantum will not need to display any features passed on from ancestors as we have seen heredity does, since what is brought back into the fertilized egg is the power to direct, a capacity for discrimination between what will assist or hinder what the self came back to do. Through one's new life only a heightened or lowered awareness will show what one has learned in previous lives. The essence of living is carried by the quantum and its transmission is made manifest in the content of one life, including the soma one gives oneself in that life. In man, attention to what one had had cognizance of but could not realize before will show itself in the choice of natural and social environment, sex, form, involvement and activities. We already know that there may be specimens in every generation of the whole range of constellations of human behavior. The fact that this happens again and again cannot be accounted for by education at a time when we are so little knowledgeable about it — a wider scheme than that is required. To ascribe to each quantum the job of securing the conditions which one recognizes intimately will produce a more congenial environment and better chances to realize oneself, does meet the requirements with precision. Since there are so many different environments, ways of living, ways of life, opportunities, each quantum released with its awareness at work will select the constellation of conditions that best suit that awareness even before any objectivation is directed to producing what it wants.

Since mistakes are made at any level of human living, the quantum in its state before descent into an egg knows that this new life — intended to fulfill its reasons for returning in this form and into these conditions — may not quite correspond to what it reached by its own means in its previous experiment. So each conscious life will still require a full life in which to test itself and to better prepare itself for the next.

In my own case, I have been seeing more and more that in this life what has mattered most to me has been to understand. In the way set forth here. Understanding in its most general form. Not understanding of this or that. Looking back at what has happened in my life, what has mattered to me, what I have stressed and what I have ignored, I can tell myself definitely that almost everything conspired to make this possible. I see so clearly that my opting not to be involved in things I saw as possible but not as related to understanding, my acceptance of some calls rather than others, my devotion and dedication to this rather than that, have led me again and again to the awareness that this life had to be what it has been to manage to give me understanding.

Emerging within this awareness is the dim awareness that there are vast universes which are there to be perceived and that there is no longer enough time left in this life to reach them. But reaching them is becoming more important every day. The pressures of everyday life are indicating in two ways what the state of my quantum may be when I come to seek another opportunity to do what will have escaped me this time. Some pressures are being seen by me as distractions and are evaded, thus leaving no effect on my self, or are met with a minimal expenditure of energy just sufficient to feed back to me that what is being done is in the right direction and adequate to the moment.

Other pressures are being seen as awakening the awareness that the level of awareness now at work is not sufficient to allow an encounter with what is there but not yet clearly perceived. To understand that realm will take up at least one full life, starting by securing conditions which ensure that demands alien to one's realization be minimal and that opportunities come one's way to engage in some of what remains to be done thus exciting and stimulating one to accept one's conditions, while at the same time one remains alerted to the proper new calls.

When I die, I shall have gathered only that which I shall have managed to gather this life, so that there can be no mortgage of my next life by my desires and visions in this one. A complete fresh start asks that I use what is left of this life to make myself: 1) not demanding, 2) not involved in what slows me down and uses my time, 3) not engaged in doing what, from the perspective of this life, would seem needed by the next. I still need to sharpen my insights into what I have understood so far and assess in new terms where I have taken myself in my awareness, with my awareness.

However much has been welcomed of what came my way, there is still much that I could not entertain although it showed itself to me as worthwhile, and still more that I could not perceive. For this I shall have to return again and again.

To know that 13 to 18 billion years have been needed to bring the universe to where it now is, as seen by people engaged in seeing how matter evolves and that only three million of these have been used by awareness to guide us towards a better knowledge of who we are individually and collectively, gives us a temporal measure of what can be achieved to lessen the time needed for the successive layers of evolution.

Looking back at myself in this life, I see much that can only be understood if I tell my self that I must have prepared myself very thoroughly in a number of lives before this one. My way of working makes this evident and shows that it is not merely a pet idea, a makeshift approach that suits my temperament and preconceptions. In fact, I moved with great caution, slowly and watching all the time so that I would not reach a stand that merely pleased me. It took me many many years to make sure that I neither fooled myself nor would fool the others. Now, I do not mind if nobody shares what I have found, and this not minding has been integrated in my understanding of understanding and stands firmly as an awareness, neither more nor less important than many others I have managed to let come to me in this life.

When death comes, in whatever form, my quantum will use the time available for its dispersal (a billionth of a second or more) to do what the minutest particles of energy do in the universe — as we learned in our studies of radiation — that is, make itself available to be received and integrated by other energies in other forms and in certain states. There will be an egg just made where it can find a place. With this quantum added to it the egg will start using the energies available in the universe and affected by billions of years of evolution, to start afresh towards a duration on earth that will be my new life. Like this one, it will not be random, undirected, unproductive. Like this one, it will be directed by awareness, and will produce one more spell of opportunities for evolution towards greater awareness, since from this life I shall take ways of discriminating between what not to engage in as well as what to engage in, between what can easily be assimilated and what requires time to be understood. Having spent this life understanding, my self is now an understanding self and can no more lose that attribute than not be. From the start, then, my self will be in the advantageous position — at the beginning of this life it was not — of holding in its awareness the reality of each moment from conception. What will have been the results of my studies in this life will be my endowments for the next, and with such a secure beginning my self may be able to perceive the meaningful directly much earlier and more deeply, and give a density to experiencing that transforms the dim intuitions of this life into brightly lit areas for my spiritual living. Intuitions that can become explicit ways of living at a level of awareness from which I will be able to see what will call for further returns.

Like Socrates holding the hemlock and sure of releasing his quantum, I'll say at the moment of my death, "I am looking forward to what I'll be with in my next life."

Hence, let death come!

www.ingramcontent.com/pod-product-compliance
Lightning Source LLC
LaVergne TN
LVHW061225100826
845148LV00004B/865

* 9 7 8 0 8 7 8 2 5 2 4 6 6 *